All I Said Was

All I Said Was

What Every Supervisor, Employee, and Team Should Know
to Avoid Insults, Lawsuits, and the Six O'Clock News

A Practical Guide for Practical People

Michael Wade

Second edition, 2017

ISBN-13: 9781979903837
ISBN-10: 1979903832

*"You are the master
of the unspoken word."*

- ARABIAN PROVERB

"For a leader, there is no trivial comment. Something you don't remember saying may have had a devastating impact on someone who looked to you for guidance and approval. The conversation is not about the relationship; the conversation is the relationship.

- SUSAN SCOTT

*"Use your wit as a shield,
not as a dagger."*

- AMERICAN PROVERB

*"Tact is the knack of making a point
without making an enemy."*

- ISAAC ASIMOV

*"Politeness and consideration for others
is like investing pennies
and getting dollars back."*

- THOMAS SOWELL

"It's good to shut up sometimes."

- MARCEL MARCEAU

Contents

How to Use This Book

This is the revised edition of a book that first published in 2010. There is new material on how to resolve conflicts between Honesty and Caring but readers of the previous edition will find minor changes sprinkled throughout the text.

We live in an increasingly diverse society where it has become easier for well-intentioned people to insult, irritate, or offend co-workers. We also live in a litigious society where such problems can lead to lawsuits. The long-term animosities accompanying such conflicts can destroy trust and teamwork.

All I Said Was came about because, in my work as a management consultant and earlier as an EEO officer, I saw too many good people talk their way into embarrassments and disputes that could have been avoided. There were few guidelines on how to act, but plenty of second-guessers to jump on anyone who blundered. I started conducting workshops to address the problem and those classes led to this book.

For all of its emphasis on basic tact, **All I Said Was** probably won't please those who camp out at the two extremes. At one extreme can be found those callous souls who think racial slurs, sexist put-downs, and an entire range of remarks that can destroy workplace cohesion are no big deal. Of course, they usually don't have to write the big checks when their employer gets sued because of their behavior nor do they see the grimaces on the faces of their angry or injured co-workers. The other extreme is held by hypersensitive folks who can discern an insult in a compliment. They are occasionally accompanied by aggressive zealots who may be more interested in playing "gotcha" than in promoting courtesy and respect. Although such practices sadly are now common on college campuses, they have also spilled over in workplaces.

Most team members would prefer to stay away from both extremes. People don't want to work with jerks, "snowflakes" or politically correct zealots.

The book is designed to be used often. Its guidelines are short and to the point because you, the reader, are pressed for time. The subjects are organized in alphabetical order so you can jump about to find specific guidelines. It can be read quickly as a primer and easily re-read as a refresher. Although I recommend reading the entire book, you may want to skip to topics of particular interest.

So please, delve into it. Make notes. Discuss the points with your co-workers. Send me your thoughts. Argue. This is meant to spark discussions and reflection, not sanctimonious lectures.

Think of it as advice from an old friend who has seen a lot of workplace problems and who wants to spare you some pain. And please recognize that I am far from being a pillar of tactfulness. I still cringe over comments I made decades ago!

Michael Wade
Phoenix, 2017

Accusations: When to Ignore

There are times when no matter what you do, you can count on being misinterpreted. For example, one communication study indicated that if you remain silent when an accusation is hurled in your general direction, then many people will interpret your failure to protest your innocence as a sign of guilt. The same study, however, noted that many other people take exactly the opposite view and regard any vigorous protest on your part as a sign that you are guilty. They believe that you're upset because the accusation stuck a nerve.

So what should you do? Watch out for knee-jerk responses. If you do believe a denial is appropriate, then give the context of your reply, such as "I'd normally ignore that allegation because it doesn't really apply to me, but since many people may view silence as a form of admission, I will make this observation" and then briefly state why the accusation is without merit.

Apologize: How to

If you are going to apologize, do so without reservation. Don't toss in loopholes. Some examples of inadequate apologies are:

"I'm sorry if I offended you." [What do you mean by "If"? You know you offended the other person. That's why you're apologizing.]

"If my words were taken in a manner that I did not intend...." [This is even worse. Translation: "If you are so dense that you missed my meaning...."]

What's the best approach? Direct and with sincerity: "I'm sorry. I acted poorly and I deeply regret it."

Do not add lengthy explanations that may dilute the message. Make it clear and unequivocal. When the legendary New York City Mayor Fiorello LaGuardia was reminded that he had made an embarrassing political appointment, he quickly diffused the problem by declaring, "When I make a mistake, it's a beaut."

Battles: Pick Them Carefully

Have you ever encountered a person who interrupted another to correct a mistake in grammar or pronunciation? There are some occasions where that may be justified, such as when the correction is to save the person from embarrassment at an upcoming speech or meeting, but in most instances the correction itself is a blunder.

Why? Because what you regard as constructive criticism will be seen by the other person as simply criticism. It is a form of "gotcha." ·

Presidential speechwriter James Humes recalled a 1967 meeting in which a general told then-former president Dwight Eisenhower, "Herodotus said about the Peloponnesian War, 'You cannot be an armchair general 28 miles from the front.'"

Eisenhower replied, "Well, that's interesting. Herodotus. The Peloponnesian War."

Afterwards, Mr. Humes asked Eisenhower where the quotation came from and President Eisenhower said, "First of all, it wasn't Herodotus. It was Aemilius Paullus. Secondly, it wasn't the Peloponnesian War. It was the Punic Wars with Carthage." He also noted that the man had misquoted. When Humes asked why Eisenhower didn't correct the man, Ike replied, "I got where I did by knowing when to hide my ego and hide my intelligence."

Bigot: Sounding Like a

Okay, you're not a racist or a sexist or whatever. Let's take that as granted. But do you sound like one? That is the suspicion which arises when someone uses terms or humor with echoes of the bad, old days. Even people who believe that you are not guilty of evil intent will question your choice of words. It is no fun to be in the position of arguing, "Hey, I'm not a racist. I just sound like one!"

One of the subtle ways of triggering suspicion of bias is when a person uses language that reflects a negative stereotype. Mention a person's race, ethnicity, religion or age and then couple that with an observation that the person either represents that group or is an exception to what may be expected from that group and you can rapidly get on thin ice.

Consider the assumption behind the following line:

"Tom, though in his sixties, plays tennis twice a week."
[Implication: People in their sixties are infirm.]

It is easy for such assumptions to slip into our language. Most of us carry a bag of prejudices that has been filled over the years. There can even be truth in many of them. [People in their sixties usually aren't as fit as those in their twenties.] That is a good reason for periodically checking out our assumptions and especially the implications of our remarks. It should also inspire a hesitation to criticize when someone else says something that might have an unintended implication.

Bragging Rights...and Wrongs

Any diverse workplace will have people who feel that bragging isn't offensive if you can actually accomplish a particular task and others who believe that bragging is never appropriate. That's why football players who do a victory dance after scoring a touchdown will trigger wildly different reactions from the audience. What one may see as exuberance, another will regard as grandstanding.

The safest strategy: Be conservative with your own bragging and forgiving with people who do brag. They may not even think they are bragging.

Business before Pleasure?

That's the general rule in the United States, but it's not always the best one. Many cultures want to know you as a person before jumping to business. A little coffee, a little small talk, and eventually the meeting will drift around to the main purpose of its existence. You'll find the same approach resonates with many of your co-workers.

You shouldn't use this during emergencies - don't serve tea before treating sucking chest wounds - and the socializing doesn't need to be lengthy, but inserting a little socializing time can add to your effectiveness.

On any given day any person can make a persuasive pitch, but people are more than the sum of their arguments.

The other person wants to know who you are and, more importantly, that you value him or her as a person and not just as a transaction.

Business Cards: Accepting and Giving

The exchanging of business cards is a common ritual but it is a ritual. While it doesn't approach the Japanese Tea Ceremony in its intricacy, certain rules apply. Here are the key ones:

Don't offer your business card unless the other person asks for it or your card is clearly needed. Some sales representatives give their cards to anything that fogs a mirror. By doing so, they only make themselves look desperate. They miss the obvious fact that it is more important to get the prospect's card than the other way around.

Only give one card unless the other person has requested more. They are not your PR firm.

Never give a card that is out of date or is soon to be obsolete. Get the other person's card and then e-mail the new information.

When accepting another person's card, take the time to read it carefully. Many executives are familiar with the Japanese custom of taking the other person's card with both hands, reading it, and commenting on the title or appearance. Americans and many other nationalities won't be so formal, but at the same time, quickly tucking the card into a pocket or briefcase may be seen as abrupt. Often, people are inordinately proud of their business cards and they hate to see them treated like a piece of scrap paper.

Call Waiting

The "call waiting" option on telephones can be an advanced way of telling people that their conversation just dropped in priority and someone else is more deserving of your attention. This is sometimes understandable. You may have been waiting on a high priority call or a person may have called who never calls unless it is an emergency. Aside from those exceptions, "call waiting" abuse is simply rude.

Consider this before you tell someone that his or her priority just dropped: Would you do it to your boss?

Calm Down: Never Tell an Upset Person to

That only increases the anger or frustration. You are, in effect, accusing the person of being irrational or out of control. None of us likes to be either of those. We also don't care to be lectured to and the "Calm down" message says, "I'm in control and you're not."

What are some alternatives? Although it is not appropriate for all scenarios, "Let's collect our thoughts and meet in five minutes" can work wonders. [Besides, if you're dealing with an upset person, you may need to collect your own thoughts.]

When the person has good cause to be angry, you can make a major step toward defusing the situation by agreeing; e.g., "I can certainly understand why you're upset." The acknowledgement that the person has good cause to be upset puts you and the other person on the same team. It is then possible to explore if the two of you can agree on a way to resolve the issue.

Cell Phones and Text-Messaging

Pretend that you are speaking at a meeting, workshop, or conference. You are about to reach a particularly emotional or important part of your presentation, one where you hope to have the full attention of your audience, and just then, someone's cell phone goes off. The moment is lost. The group is treated to the William Tell Overture as the offender fumbles about to turn the darned thing off. [The worst offenders, of course, are those who actually take the call and remain in the room. Visions of flogging come to mind.]

Turn off your cell phone or put it on "vibrate" during such events. Remember that some phones that are off will still ring if the ringer is on! If you are in a meeting and are expecting an important call, you should apologize and tell the other participants of your situation. It is wise to sit in the back near the door so you can make a smooth exit without being disruptive.

Do not underestimate the irritation level of people who are subjected to listening to another person talk on a cell phone.

Text-messaging when someone else is talking to you is simply rude. Many young people regard text-messaging during conversations as acceptable. They and their peers may see nothing disrespectful, but that opinion is not shared by people from other generations. [Believe me. I hear those complaints.] Why engage in behavior that is unnecessary, can detract from your ability to listen, and will be viewed as discourteous by many of your associates?

Chain of Command: Following the

In many hierarchical organizations, not following the chain of command is a major sin. Your immediate supervisor should be your first contact if a problem arises that you cannot handle and which requires assistance from a higher-up. This doesn't mean that you should pester your supervisor with minor matters that you could resolve on your own. It does mean that you should determine which items you 'd be expected to kick upstairs.

All jobs have a triage: Decisions you should make on your own, decisions that should be made only after consultation with your supervisor, and decisions that are solely the province of your supervisor or someone else further up the chain.

Naturally, there are exceptions. If your supervisor is not available and the matter is an emergency, then use your best judgment but promptly report the matter to your boss as soon as the dust settles. If your supervisor is the problem – he's a harasser or she makes a point of waving around a revolver – then you can jump the chain and talk to your boss's boss or go directly to the folks in Human Resources.

In general, honor the chain of command. Doing so is both efficient and fair.

Comparisons: Unwise or Insensitive

A basketball game announcer calls a lopsided score a "holocaust." A rock singer says that she'd like to be thin like the starving children in Africa but preferably without the flies and death and stuff. A senator compares his support of a political deal to the courage displayed by soldiers in combat.

Before pointing in derision, consider how easily even extraordinary diplomats (such as the two of us!) can slip into a cloddish mode. Remember this simple rule: Don't compare your own troubles to those of a famous event or person.

You aren't Moses, Jesus, or Job.

Complaints: Don't Delay

S toring grievances and then emptying the entire "gunny sack" on the offender is unhealthy and unwise. Gunny sacking is the revenge of the procrastinator. It is often used by mellow people whose patience has finally expired.

By not promptly confronting the matter, you not only suffer the stress of carrying around the complaints, you also experience a workplace in which a multitude of problems has been unaddressed. Even if the offender suspected that you might have had a problem, the passage of time has signaled that the matter was not that great or else you would have spoken up.

There are some areas of employee conflict, such as harassment, in which people are reluctant to declare their discomfort. The best practice in such cases is to report the problem to the employer as soon as possible. That is usually the quickest way to get the matter resolved. If you are the victim and the employer does not have a credible complaint procedure, then contact the appropriate government civil rights enforcement agencies. Do not sit back and expect things to get better.

Condescension: Talking Down and Dressing Down

Have you ever heard a politician who has been coached to speak as if voters can only comprehend at the level of a third grader? It is not very enjoyable, is it? You want to know the person's views on international terrorism and he or she sounds like a camp counselor reading "The Cat in the Hat." Audiences appreciate being taken seriously and when they hear kid-speak they just feel they are being taken for fools.

The same rule applies to dress. I once had an assignment to train a large group of blue-collar workers on harassment prevention. One of the executives, noting my coat and tie, advised me to dress more informally. His heart was in the right place, but his advice wasn't. If I'd gone out there in blue jeans and an open collar those workers would have immediately thought, "Phony." They would have known that I do not normally dress that way for workshops and since there was no other reason for informal wear, such as crawling through a tunnel or walking around a cotton field, my informal dress would have signaled that I was pretending to be just one of the guys. [It reminds me of a line by comedian Mitch Hedberg: "I used to be a hot-tar roofer. Yeah, I remember that day."]

Sincerity is far more important. By dressing my usual way I also handled another unspoken fact: They didn't want to be taught by just one of the guys. They wanted the same guy who'd taught the executives. And they got him.

Confrontation

Most of us do not like conflict. We would prefer to pass on the hassle and unpleasantness that can be part of a serious confrontation. Consequently, either we remain silent or we hint and hope that the offender will catch on. This rarely works.

If you have concluded that you need to confront someone about something they have said, here are some lines that can be used according to the level of offense:

"Let's raise the level of conversation."

"We don't talk like that around here."

"I'm going to talk politely with you but if you want me to be part of this conversation you'll have to do the same with me."

"I have no problems with you overall as a professional. There is one specific thing, however, I'd like you to change."

"You really harm your reputation and effectiveness when you use language like that."

"I don't think you are prejudiced but when you use terms like that you sound like a bigot."

"Please tell me what you meant by that remark. What are you really trying to say?"

"I want to tell you how I feel whenever you ...."

Make sure that you focus on the remark and not on their motives or personality. Choose a time and setting that will reduce the chance of interruptions.

Recognize that by talking about how you feel, you shift the conversation to a point that cannot be disputed. People may argue that you should not feel a particular way, but they cannot dispute that you do feel that way. You are the only authority on your feelings.

As unpleasant as it can be to confront people, many offenders count on never being confronted. When they are called on their remarks, they back off. If the person does not back off, however, at least you have stated your position.

People can get downright paranoid when they learn that you pushed or made a decision pertaining to their turf and did not consult them in advance. We all want to feel important and failing to coordinate decisions or actions is seen as a statement that the omitted person does not count.

The safest approach is to err on the side of excessive coordination. For example, if you are proposing a particular course of action and are circulating a staff paper or scheduling a meeting on that decision, if there is any hint that the Widget Department might have an interest in the subject, be sure to include them. It is far better to risk that they will bring in some superfluous insights than it is to chance ticking them off.

Credit: Giving

Be generous in giving credit to others. Not only is it the right thing to do, it has the added impact of motivating others and fostering your image as a person who notices the contributions of others.

Hogging the credit has no real upside. For every person who claimed undue credit on a project and subsequently reaped huge benefits, many more lost the trust of co-workers and gained the scorn of superiors. We all cringe at the Academy Award winners who thank everyone who helped him or her since kindergarten, but they are on to something. It is much better to over-thank than to under-acknowledge.

Customers: Handling Upset

H ere is a general rule for handling upset customers: Your interaction should not make matters worse. If that sounds obvious, it must have escaped many a front desk or call center employee because their approach to customer relations often inflames instead of soothes.

Your first strategy is to show empathy. (Customer relations guru Jeffrey Gitomer suggests, "Oh, that's horrible!" as a way of letting the customer know you care.) You then can move to solving the problem. Gitomer describes a scenario in which he tried to make an appointment at a recording studio and the employee said, "You can't do it until Friday. We're booked solid until then. We can't take you." He contrasts it with this response: "Jeffrey, you're in luck! I've got a spot open on Friday."

You can imagine how you would respond to the different wording.

What you do not want to do is to fall into these roles:

Uncaring bureaucrat: "Our policy is...."
Busy server: "That's not my table (responsibility)."
Clueless lackey: "I don't know how to do that."

Your emphasis should be on caring and helping. This does not mean that you can give away the store, but that you demonstrate a concern for the customer's problem, a willingness to make things better, and action to show that is sincere.

Decor: Questionable

A client of mine, a company that worked in the agricultural industry, had a series of prints in its lobby. Each picture depicted the cotton fields of the South, which was perfectly understandable because their product was linked to cotton. Unfortunately, every one of the pictures also had another component: Blacks picking cotton.

Being a natural art critic, I suggested that they replace the pictures with something more modern.

Now I know that some folks would call that being overly sensitive and yet for a company that was reaching out to recruit more African Americans in order to get past its "good ole boy" image, those prints presented the wrong image.

The Sports Illustrated Swimsuit edition is extremely clever marketing and I suspect that most women can see one without frothing about sexism, but that does not mean a calendar of those photos is a wise choice for your work desk. Ask yourself this: If there was a chance that I would lose a major contract or offend a major customer by having that on my desk, would I still keep it there? You know the answer.

Office decor, like business dress, should be such that it does not become a barrier to the conduct of business. Once it does, it is a problem.

Devil's Advocate: Playing

If you are going to play the devil's advocate and critique another's ideas or proposals, then do so with sensitivity and without glee. The minute you begin to enjoy the task, you may be creating an enemy.

That is a reason for rotating the devil's advocate assignment. When one person is continually saddled with the role, he or she risks being ostracized and labeled.

No matter how often the criticism is described as "constructive," some will sense that the constructive part is well hidden. They may be correct. Constructive criticism can be an oxymoron - like jumbo shrimp and tight slacks – and the best way to downplay its negativity is to focus on clarifying the strengths and weaknesses of a proposal or project instead of determining whether it is good or bad. Clarification is non-threatening. It is constructive. Placing options on a good or bad scale creates an adversarial climate.

Seek clarity, not victory.

Direct: Being Too

Being direct is not always bad. There are many indirect people who are so obtuse that they seldom clearly communicate. Certainly, there are moments when a good direct statement is best. Diplomacy has its limits.

People who are too direct, however, can be like truck drivers who only use one gear. They create more problems than they resolve because in their focus on getting the message across, they miss the importance of keeping a cohesive team of enthusiastic supporters. People do not expect softness, but they do want basic courtesy. If you think of yourself as a very direct person, don't pat yourself on the back. In order to be effective, you should have the ability to shift back and forth between directness and a more indirect approach when the situation demands. It may feel good to be direct, but it is better to be effective.

Disputes: Engaging in

Management prefers peace over justice. Firing off harsh memos will not score points and refusing to cooperate with a co-worker can be a ticket to oblivion.

People who act like spoiled stars are more likely to be regarded as spoiled than catered to as stars. As political speechwriter Vic Gold once put it, "The squeaky wheel is sometimes replaced." The wisest strategy in any workplace dispute is to seize the high ground by being as reasonable as possible.

Let the other person play prima donna. You may have some short-term losses but you'll gain over the long term, especially as a person. To paraphrase an old joke, you don't want to win the rat race if it means becoming a rat.

Disrespect: Little Acts of

Disrespect is seldom shown in large, messy acts of insubordination or rudeness. It is revealed in the little acts that slowly chip away at trust. Here are some little acts of disrespect that can seriously harm your reputation:

Not returning phone calls.

Not being on time.

Changing agreed-upon plans and not telling the other person about the change.

Failing to coordinate with or consult.

Speaking another language in front of others who don't understand that language.

Over-promising.

Missing deadlines.

Not giving appropriate credit.

Failing to provide reasonable support.

If you've done any of these, see **Apologize: How to**.

E-mail: Dos and Don'ts

Never send an e-mail when you are angry. E-mail messages are one of the first bits of evidence that plaintiff attorneys seek in employment lawsuits nowadays and one reason is they tend to be high on emotion and low on discretion. E-mail should not be used for sensitive topics - one company received terrible publicity when it sent lay-off notices to employees via e-mail - and nothing should be put in an e-mail that you would not feel comfortable seeing on the front page of the newspaper.

Due to their brevity, e-mail messages can come across as abrupt or rude. Before sending a message, re-read it to ensure that the appropriate tone is being conveyed. Always consider if the topic can be handled more effectively via the telephone or a face-to-face meeting.

Explanations: You're on Defense

If you have to explain, you're in trouble. You are playing defense and most people do not look good when they are bobbing, weaving, and redefining the meaning of the word "is." If your actions are not self-explanatory, your cause may not be lost, but you'd better be able to give a quick and persuasive justification without the use of flow charts and footnotes.

A prominent cancer medical center was criticized after it sent out a community survey to determine why black women were not having routine medical exams. Unfortunately, the survey asked whether the respondents agreed with statements such as:

> "I eat chitlins once in a while."
> "Deep in their heart, most white people are racist."
> "I believe that some people know how to use voodoo."

After receiving significant criticism from the community, the medical center scrambled to regain credibility. Its convoluted justifications for the survey only seemed to make matters worse.

Expressions that Offend

Our language contains a sordid array of phrases and terms that can pose problems. These vary from the extremely offensive to the potentially embarrassing. Among them are:

Deaf and dumb
Wetback
Chinese fire drill
Bastard
Paddy wagon
Welshed on a bet, Indian giver, Gypped
Wheelchair bound
Free, white and 21
White Trash, Trailer Trash, Redneck
Jesus·Freak, Bible Thumper
Off the reservation, Circle the wagons
Cripple

There are certain terms to which some group members won't object – I know of a person who uses a wheelchair who doesn't hesitate to describe himself as a "cripple" and many whites call themselves "rednecks" - but the use of any of these will put you within range of criticism.

Eye Contact

It is best to avoid the extremes when making eye contact. Some people, possibly because of shyness or cultural reasons, will avoid eye contact while others zero in as if you have turned into a space alien.

Some of us – I'll place myself in this category – will avert our eyes as we think of a profound response but eventually we return to the conversation, assuming the other person is still in the room.

Here are some simple strategies:

Consider whether your own eye contact makes others uncomfortable. Your review may reveal that it only makes certain people uneasy. If so, you need to increase or decrease your eye contact when dealing with those individuals.

If staring right into a person's eyes is undesirable, focus on the point just between their eyebrows. It will give the same effect.

Men: If women keep flashing their engagement or wedding rings and talking about their significant others, that may be a sign that your eye contact is a tad too intense.

Women: If men start tugging at their shirt collar, your eye contact may pose the same problem.

Rather than telling Karl that he doesn't care for the lengthy written reports that Karl turns in each month, Harold pretends to find them useful when he is really just throwing them away. When Karl learns of the deception, he feels like a fool. Trust is shattered even though Harold may have been trying to avoid hurting Karl's feelings.

I have used "Fibs" instead of "Lies" as the title for this section because fibs are regarded as less serious than lies. That can be a dodge. It may be too tempting to justify a lie by dressing it up as a fib. The person who is deceived may see little merit in such distinctions.

Setting aside extreme circumstances, the best ground rule to follow is that Truth will trump Caring. You can try to deliver the truth as gently as possible, but even if there is some short-term pain that pain will be less harmful than the damage your credibility will suffer if you are caught in a well-meaning lie, fib, dodge, or fudge.

It is better to have a reputation for being blunt than one for being slippery. Grit your teeth, but tell the truth.

Flirting

When only one party is flirting, it is unprofessional.

When both parties are flirting and each is serious, it may be a prelude to an affair as well as being unprofessional.

When both parties are flirting and only one is serious, it is a formula for heartache.

When each of the above scenarios occurs in the workplace, co-workers can be irritated and favoritism may be suspected. The first scenario may even spark a harassment complaint.

Is it really worth it?

Generation Gaps and Insults

One of the signs of progress in the battle against bigotry is that many of the racial stereotypes of the past are unknown to members of the younger generation. In comparison to the Thirties and Forties, where offensive racial stereotypes were frequently found in cartoons, stage plays, and movies, today's society is remarkably enlightened. We've traveled a long way from those days.

This progress, however, can produce situations in which young people make comments that evoke an offensive stereotype while remaining completely unaware that their words carry a historically negative connotation. While that may inspire greater study of race relations, it should also restrain any quick conclusions that every stereotypical remark is ill intended.

Gift Giving

Many organizations have guidelines on gift giving, mainly to prevent ethical problems that may arise when vendors hand out goodies to curry favor. Even if a gift does not come with an ulterior motive, it may simply be inappropriate. Beware of the following:

Gifts that may create cultural problems. If you are giving a present to a person from another nationality or culture, you should check out books and resources on intercultural communication to see if there is a problem. (For example, in China giving a clock is an offensive reminder of mortality.)

Gifts that are unduly familiar, such as intimate apparel, romantic publications, or anything else with a sexual connotation, should be avoided. Not only may those be interpreted as an advance, they may embarrass the other person.

Gifts that are too expensive may create the impression that the other person is expected to reciprocate at some point with a present of similar value. Stressing that the other person does not need to do so may be interpreted as a signal that the other person cannot afford to do so. There can even be a rising expectations problem: The recipient may expect that your next gift will be equally lavish.

Gifts that are tacky or cheap. Unless the idea is to give a "joke gift," it is better to pass on giving a gift at all than to give one that resembles a donation to a rummage sale. An exception: Some item that will have a particular appeal for the recipient. For example, an old, used, book of poetry may be a treasured item if the person is an avid fan of the poet. If you have any reservation about giving a particular gift, explore your feelings. Your mind may be signaling you that there is an inappropriate aspect.

One tip: Keep a list of gifts that you have given. Why? The more gifts you give over the years, the harder it can be to remember if you have already given the same gift to a person.

Gossiping: Not a Minor Offense

Let's set aside the harmless gossip such as whether or not a reorganization is in the wind and instead focus on harmful gossip where negative or hurtful things are said. The most dysfunctional groups with whom I have worked as a consultant have been torn apart by harmful gossip. Otherwise responsible men and women spent part of each workday shoveling dirt about their co-workers. In several cases, the co-workers were reciprocating. What should have been a workplace resembled a high school cafeteria. No one gained by the gossip epidemic unless you count the lawyers who eventually handled the mess.

Charles Colson, who served time in prison in the wake of the Watergate scandal, later observed, "I've discovered that all the guys we thought were our friends weren't so good and all the guys we thought were our enemies weren't so bad." Harmful gossiping is not a minor offense. Its corrosive effects can destroy careers and reputations. Leaders and followers alike should squelch gossip whenever possible.

Gotcha: Playing

There are people who are inclined to find an insult in even the most innocent of remarks or behavior. Some squander huge amounts of time wondering about motives. Others walk into workplaces with the notion that their co-workers and boss will be bigoted or unfair and, to no real surprise, they find what they suspected. These hypersensitive characters can poison the workplace's atmosphere and destroy team cohesion.

If you want people to cut you some slack, you should do the same for them. Don't play "gotcha." If you supervise a hypersensitive person, uphold reasonable standards and don't let the person's "gotcha" game create a climate of fear in which others are afraid to speak.

Gunny Sacking

This is a common management infraction. Instead of dealing with an employee performance problem when it arises, the supervisor tucks it into a mental "gunny sack." Once the sack has become sufficiently full or the employee does something especially irritating, the supervisor walks in and dumps the sack on the employee's desk; i.e. the employee gets bombarded with allegations of misconduct or poor performance going back weeks or even months.

Employees reasonably resent this technique because it goes to the heart of whether they can trust the supervisor. After all, the supervisor has been behaving as if there were no problem and then suddenly it turns out that the supervisor's earlier demeanor was all an act. Employees sometimes play this same game. Either way, it's offensive.

And there's a simple solution: Don't gunny sack your concerns. Have a prompt and honest discussion about them with the other party.

Handshakes

Reasonable pressure combined with a direct look into the person's eyes and then a release of the palm.

That is the gold standard of handshakes.

Consider what it is not. It doesn't mean that the other person's hand is taken in a vise-like grip as if you are trying to win some test of strength at the State Fair. It doesn't mean that your hand is so limp that it resembles a dead fish. Nor should you fail to release the other person's palm; an action that immediately triggers primal defense reactions as the individual feels like a diver trapped by a giant clam.

People are occasionally flustered if they meet a person whose disability has deformed a hand. My advice: Shake the deformed hand without hesitation. When Senator Robert Dole ran for president, many people, remembering that the Senator's right arm was injured in war, would extend their left hand. That was a graceful gesture that you could tell Dole appreciated.

And that is what a handshake should be: a sign of courtesy and friendliness.

Happy Hour

Do you really believe that you can go off-site to a Happy Hour, act like an oaf with your co-workers or, worse yet, people you supervise, and not have that affect the way you are perceived at work?

You may think that you can build a Berlin Wall between those moments and your professional life, but you are sadly fooling yourself. Those moments can become legendary; the subject of many a whispered conversation and even the main focus of retirement parties.

If you have stumbled badly during such an event, I suggest that you address it directly with your associates. You don't need to grovel or groan, but you should directly and seriously vow, "I'll never do that again."

And then don't.

Harassment versus Rites of Passage

A military boot camp is a rite of passage. It's tough. Highly demanding. But it is also controlled and conducted by professionals. It has a definite beginning and a definite end and follows set rules. Those who get through it are warmly admitted into the ranks of the chosen.

Harassment is very different. Its goal is not to include, but to exclude. There is no hope for the victim because there is no end in sight. It is not controlled by professionals, there are no set rules, and its actions are designed to demean, not toughen.

Don't try to dress up harassment as a rite of passage. And never pretend that preventing harassment is someone else's responsibility. It is everyone's responsibility.

Holiday Greetings

I'm going to be blunt: Anyone who gets offended because another person gives a wish for a Merry Christmas or Happy Hanukkah or Ramadan or whatever the religious holiday may be... needs to lighten up. A person is wishing you happiness and you are offended? Now if the greeting is done in a way that is a putdown for a nonbeliever or if actual religious discrimination is present, that is another matter. In 99% of the cases, however, the greeting itself is not meant to offend and no offense should be taken.

People may argue that the greeting presumes that you are a follower of that particular religion. That is a stretch. You can say Happy Halloween or Happy New Year to people without assuming that they celebrate either holiday. (I've known Europeans who dislike the American habit of saying, "Have a good day." They groan that they will have whatever sort of day they choose to have and they don't need any cheery Yanks telling them how to behave. There, there, now. Have a cup of herbal tea and a trained counselor will be with you soon.) But since we're exploring implicit messages, consider this one: By wishing a person the politically-correct Happy Holiday – and which soulless apparachik thought up that phrase? - am I not possibly inferring that the individual is so ultra-sensitive that hearing "Merry Christmas" will be taken as an insult? That by itself may be more grating than any religious greeting.

Hygiene, Cologne, Perfume, and Other Smells

I saw a person clear out a training room one time by eating a hard boiled egg over the break. The rest of the class did not return until the place had been aired out.

Powerful colognes and perfumes can have similar effects and can send the message that the wearer is unsophisticated. [The more subtle the fragrance, the better the reaction.] People with allergies may also be troubled by strong scents.

Hygiene is an even more sensitive topic but it goes right to the basics. Daily showers, clean hair, clean clothes, mouthwash, and the use of deodorant are not too much to ask.

If in Doubt, Don't

Whenever anyone asks me, "Do you think it will be okay if I tell this joke at my staff meeting?" I always stop them and immediately reply, "If you are worried enough to ask me, then it's not okay."

That rule goes for any behavior. If your conscience is telling you that something might not be right, it probably isn't. Your mind is sending a danger signal.

Do not discount the logic of your intuition.

Having said that, let me note that the "If in doubt, don't" rule is mainly justified by the "lawyerization" of our society. I worry more than a little bit that our conversations may become so sanitized and filtered that we risk becoming "pre-emptive wimps." It is as if everyone is running for office and each word must always be carefully weighed. A hyper-sanitized workplace is not necessarily a healthy one. The self-censorship may indicate a huge lack of trust.

Ignoring Ideas

During the meeting, Yolanda brought up the idea of selling the old office equipment. It was promptly ignored by the other participants until, ten minutes later, Jack proposed the same thing. At that point, people started to praise the option. Jack beams. Yolanda fumes or is hurt.

This is a common complaint of women in many organizations and yet I've also seen men who don't fit an organization's favorite profile (young, attractive, extroverted, and articulate) receive the same treatment. Bias may be the culprit but poor listening skills can also play a role.

Solution? Become a note-taker and keep track of who says what. Listen carefully for areas of overlap and distinguishing factors - some proposals may sound alike but may have slight yet meaningful differences – but always give credit to the person who first surfaced the idea. It is both good management and basic courtesy.

If you are not a member of a group, your joking rights are not the same as the group members. Sure, some racial or ethnic group members discriminate against others from the same group, but the general view is that insiders are less likely to do so. That is why outsiders are judged by a higher standard.

A group loyalty may also be triggered by an outsider's comments. (Most of us resent it when strangers criticize our relatives. That's our job!)

Should racial slurs be tolerated by anyone? Never. And people who use the very slurs that have been historically used against their own groups (Rap singers: Listen up!) are helping to reduce a stigma that should be firmly attached to those terms.

Interrupting: Not

Some cultures have the rule of never interrupting. Others permit interrupting if the information is relevant. Others have long gaps of silence between the statement and the response. The differences can be as dramatic as the contrast between the conversations at a boisterous Italian American family dinner and those at a relatively quiet Navajo gathering.

Since "not interrupting" is not a communication sin and interrupting may be, the safest approach is to avoid interrupting and to accept silence. Not every conversational gap needs to be filled. Listening means absorbing the other person's message and not silently preparing your response.

Irrational Comments

Psychologist George Miller originated what is known as Miller's Rule: "In order to understand what another person is saying, you must assume that to be true and try to imagine what it could be true of."

Come again? I'll give an example. I was in a meeting with some police officers about some personnel issues when one of the officers made a statement that seemed to be completely bonkers. After the initial desire to order drug testing was quietly considered and ruled out, I asked him to elaborate on the reasons for his position. It turned out that, given certain assumptions, he thought our impressive safeguards were hollow and ineffective. If I had held his assumptions, I would have reached the same conclusions.

When someone appears to be acting irrationally, remember that in that person's world, the behavior is rational. Your job as a communicator is to find out why.

Joking

I once heard an employment law attorney recommend having a bland workplace in which there was no joking or teasing. He had an ulterior motive, of course. He wanted to make it easier to prevent and defend against harassment claims.

That may make life sweet for the lawyers, but I would hate to work in a bland workplace. Productivity would suffer and employee morale would be in the basement.

What we need to do is to squeeze out the cruelty and keep the good-natured humor. Chief Alan Brunacini of the Phoenix Fire Department once noted, "Every firefighter can remember, with painful clarity, situations where their feelings were hurt by co-workers – in some cases, 30 – 40 years earlier. Generally, those who hurt their feelings were people they looked up to, and many were individuals the harmed person expected (by virtue of their rank, seniority or stature) would protect them."

Humor that hurts ceases to be humorous. Watching out for the cruel quip that may be painfully remembered years from now does not mean that you cannot joke. It simply means that you should joke with the restraint of common sense.

Joking and Mixed Company

Jokes can cover a great deal of territory when it comes to their propriety. In general, if you cannot tell a joke in mixed company in the workplace, you should not tell it at all.

Inherently offensive humor – as opposed to that which is mildly inappropriate – is never appropriate. Aside from revealing a lack of professionalism and taste, such remarks are trust-killers.

The idea that you can foster an atmosphere of - and reputation for - trust while telling racist, sexist, or homophobic jokes is absurd. As a minority male in a workplace investigation once told me, "The [sexist] jokes are never told in front of the women, but I always wonder what they say when I walk out of the room."

Law: Don't Just Comply with the

I'm never impressed when managers and supervisors tell me that they obey the law. Obeying the law is a pretty low standard. You can engage in a lot of shabby behavior and not violate the law. You can also drive a lot of your employees and co-workers to the local enforcement agencies.

Be sure to obey the law, but also set a higher standard in which basic courtesy and respect are always accorded. This should even apply in contentious situations. As U.S. Supreme Court Justice Potter Stewart once noted, "Ethics is knowing the difference between what you have a right to do, and what is the right thing to do."

Doing the right thing is not only ethical. It is also wise. In most cases, it will put you in safe territory and far away from the boundary line that separates the legal from the illegal.

Leadership by Example

Leadership by example is important for a reason: People will pay more attention to your behavior than to your policy pronouncements. You can't behave like a monster on Monday and deliver a credible speech about courtesy on Tuesday.

If you are in a position of responsibility, you are the bird and your employees are the bird watchers. Every habit, gesture, and remark is studied. You are the subject of many a luncheon conversation. Act hypocritically and your employees will spot it immediately.

What if you have to act hypocritically due to the nature of your responsibilities? Charles de Gaulle once noted, "There are many things I would have liked to do but could not, for they would not have been fitting for General de Gaulle." He knew that there are times when hypocrisy may be required due to your role.

Some guidelines: Let your actions match your words. Do what you say you will do. Take care of your employees before taking care of yourself.

You are not an independent operator. You cannot be just yourself because your job is more than your feelings and whims. You have a role to play, relationships to maintain, and responsibilities to fulfill.

Listening

Listening is one of the greatest compliments that you can give to an individual. You are declaring that the person is worthy of your time and attention. It is not, however, a skill that comes naturally. Like public speaking, it must be learned and practiced. When listening:

Listen for what the person means, not just what is said. A changed tone or a certain word can indicate a very different meaning than the strict definition of the words. Lazy listeners focus only on the words. Effective listeners focus on the total message. The words may say things are fine but the eyes may indicate trouble.

Watch the other person's body language, but also watch your own. If you are slouched in a manner that indicates disinterest, the other person will sense that, shorten the message, and prematurely end the conversation. Your poor posture can affect the amount and clarity of the information that you receive.

Pretend to listen. Scoot forward in your chair. Establish eye contact. Act as if you are listening and – surprise – you will start to listen.

Get rid of distractions. Music, phone calls, and other interruptions can distract. This is no time for multitasking.

Ask questions for clarification. Summarize points. "So, as I understand it, what you are saying is...."

Use contrasting: "And you're not saying that...."

Avoid interrupting. Aside from being discourteous, it may be viewed as an indication that you are not listening.

If you are listening to a person's account of an event, such as during an investigation, let the person tell about it without interruption, then go over the facts in reverse chronological order. This can help to jar the person's memory and it is much more effective than simply "rewinding the tape" on what has been said.

50

Location

A supervisor tells an employee, "May I see you in my office?" The employee immediately thinks, "Uh oh."

The supervisor may intend to praise the employee or to talk about something minor and yet the employee thinks he's in trouble. After all, bad things happen when you are summoned to the supervisor's office.

The problem could have been headed off if the supervisor had identified the subject of the meeting or had chosen a neutral location, such as a conference room or a coffee shop.

Match the location with the subject. A coffee shop would be inappropriate for a confidential discussion. Going to the employee's office can be a savvy choice. Aside from being less threatening, doing so permits the supervisor to end the meeting easily by simply leaving. [If that sounds strange, consider this: Have you ever gotten someone in your office and then had to struggle to get him or her to leave?]

Loudness

A surprising number of people complain about loud co-workers. They are trying to make a phone call or are meeting with an employee and Foghorn Leghorn down the hall is talking about his fishing trip. No one can concentrate. His voice can cut iron.

"Haw, haw," he goes on. "And then the bait...Did I tell you about the bait?"

He's told everyone within shouting distance about the bait.

If you are a loud person, God bless you. Some people are just loud. Their voices carry. But you need to recognize that you are loud and what may seem like a soft-spoken tone to you is probably normal to anyone else. Just as some folks need to speak up, you need to tone down. Work on it and, whenever possible, move your conversations away from the open area and into a closed office.

We've already heard about the bait.

Meetings can sometimes bring out the worst in people. Strive to avoid the following infractions:

Arriving late.

Arriving late and making noise as you find a seat.

Arriving unprepared when you were expected to have completed some "homework."

Taking cell phone calls or text-messaging during the meeting.

Acting bored.

Leaving the room at inopportune times.

Talking too much.

Not participating at all.

Reading or sending email during the meeting.

Eating odoriferous food that may clear out the room.

Smirking and whispering to other attendees.

Bringing up topics that have no relevance to the meeting's purpose.

Interrupting the presenter.

Making unreasonable demands regarding the room temperature or arrangement.

Mentoring

Many years ago, I was asked by a corporation to coach a man who'd been hit with a sexual harassment complaint by one of his employees. He was in his fifties and the young woman was in her mid-twenties.

He had started to mentor her in various aspects of the job. All of that was above board. She responded to his coaching and her work improved. The mentoring then, however, began to move into personal territory. Luncheon meetings became dinner meetings. Calls that had been made during the workday began to be made at night. Meetings were held on the weekend. At one point, he helped her with some work at her home.

Since I didn't conduct the investigation, I'm not sure if the allegations of harassment had any merit, but the man was right on target when he later told me, "I didn't realize how it would appear to others." Because mentoring is so individual and so personal, it is important to be especially careful to keep matters on a professional basis. Supervisors can easily slip into playing the role of personal counselor, a job that they are ill prepared to assume. Furthermore, when discussions become too personal, it is possible that disclosures will be made that will prejudice or destroy the professional relationship.

If mentoring, be cordial and be encouraging, but keep your distance and always be sensitive to the appearance.

Messages: Much More Than Words

Have you ever encountered a front counter worker whose words, if taken in a vacuum, were polite but whose tone indicated that you were a burden, an interruption or a dolt? Sarcasm, skepticism, insincerity and indifference are just a few of the negative emotions that you pick up in conversations.

Consider the differences that a simple change in emphasis gives to these sentences:

"***Your*** proposal was interesting." [The other proposals stunk.]

"Your ***proposal*** was interesting." [As for the rest of your work....]

"Your proposal ***was*** interesting." [But it's not anymore.]

"Your proposal was ***interesting***." [But then, train wrecks are interesting.]

The definition of your words will mean little if any reasonable person would regard the context and tone as offensive.

Mirror or Window?

Thinking that others will react or view things the same way you do is a common mistake. We improve as communicators when the other person's perspective is considered.

Does that mean we have to curb our speech to please the most hypersensitive member of our audience? Not at all. It means that we should consider the reasonable members of our audience while making certain that our definition of "reasonable" doesn't mean "Agrees with me" or "Shares my passions."

As management writer Alex McEachern advised: "No matter how much you like vegetables yourself, never try to feed a cat a carrot."

Come in and meet with me!

I can scan my e-mail, take calls, sign correspondence, order coffee, and play with my letter opener while listening to you! You'll be amazed! You'll be impressed!

Or you might conclude that I'm not really listening.

My bet is you'll think it's the second version. You'll probably say as little as possible as quickly as possible and then run away from the circus that doubles as my office.

If someone brings a question to you while you are rushing to meet a deadline, then multi-tasking may be necessary. If that's not the case, you'll pay them an enormous compliment by stopping the side-show and giving your undivided attention.

Nicknames and Titles

H.L. Mencken said the first Rotarian was the first person to call John the Baptist "Jack." You may like nicknames and disdain the use of titles, but there is a large army of people who don't share your egalitarian ways. The 80 year-olds often bristle when a sales clerk uses their first name or, worse still, a nickname.

Err on the side of formality. It will be much easier later to let your hair down than to put it back up. If you are uncertain as to which name or title a person prefers, ask, and then follow their wishes.

Office Parties: Beware of

In a Fortune magazine article, an employee summed up the danger of office parties by recalling his own memorable experience: "I drank a fair amount of Scotch on an empty stomach and I ended up dancing on a tabletop to 'She Drives Me Crazy' by the Fine Young Cannibals. For weeks after that, everyone who had been at the party started humming the tune whenever I walked into a room. It was funny but I don't think it did my career any good."

An office party resembles a real party the same way chopping your way through the Amazon rain forest resembles a stroll in the park. Just as the rain forest has an assortment of creatures who may wish you ill, your office party may contain some people who'd make a giant anaconda seem benign.

The expression, "Putting in an appearance," was made for these office events. You aren't supposed to have a good time. You're expected to show up sober, be friendly (No, not that friendly!), and then leave, preferably with your own spouse or significant other. This is especially important if you are in a management position. Stay long enough to show that you are not a snob, but not so long that you ruin the evening for those who'll give a sigh of relief when you depart.

Phrases to Use Cautiously or Not at All

Have you ever heard someone say, "To be perfectly honest" and find it causes you to wonder just how honest the person has been up to that point?

Some phrases may have the most innocent of intentions, but they spark negative reactions. Some other examples to approach cautiously are:

"Let me explain it to you."

"Well, obviously...."

"Quite frankly...."

"I don't think you understand."

Notice some **positive** contrasts:

"May I elaborate on a few points?"

"Here are some areas that are core components."

"What are your questions?"

"Are there any areas where you would like some additional detail?"

Political Discussions

It is not surprising that you can find differing guidelines regarding political discussions in the workplace. So much of the wisdom gets back to that brilliant consultant's line: It depends.

It depends upon:

The nature of the workplace. Is your organization supposed to be nonpolitical, such as a City Clerk's office? How would customers feel it they overheard the discussion?

Timing. Are emotions running too high for a calm discussion?

How well the participants know one another. Relative strangers may be more inclined to ascribe bad faith to each other.

Whether both sides are committed to maintaining a positive relationship. This commitment will strengthen civility.

Whether the participants are genuinely willing to consider other perspectives. Are they more interested in clarity than in being right?

Whether the participants can agree to disagree. Can they hear each other out without harming the team or their relationship?

How often the discussions occur. The more frequent the discussion, the greater the potential for harm.

Whether the participants can discuss matters in a polite manner in an atmosphere of mutual respect. The great jurist Learned Hand described a tone that would help many discussions when he noted: "The spirit of liberty is the spirit which is not too sure that it is right. The spirit of liberty is the spirit which seeks to understand the minds of other men and women."

If the positive elements are not present, the team may be stronger if its members save political discussions for their private lives. In most cases, that is the best practice.

Power Differences

There is a Yiddish proverb: "With money in your pocket, you are wise, and you are handsome, and you sing well too." When you are in a position of power, you enjoy the same advantage. That is why there is an invisible ripple that precedes the Chief Executive Officer as he or she strolls through a crowded office; a ripple that changes behavior and expressions in an almost magical way. The size of the ripple can depend upon your rank but it is there once you assume a position of authority.

You may never be able to remove that ripple. You can adjust for it. Don't joke and banter in a way that puts subordinates in an unequal contest. Call on the junior people first at staff meetings so you can get their opinions before the mandarins chime in. And watch out for traditional, class-ridden, distinctions such as the practice of calling secretaries or administrative assistants by their first names while everyone else is addressed more formally.

Praise: Accepting

How you ever noticed how easy it is to get some people to criticize themselves? All you have to do is praise them and they immediately tell you that the work wasn't that good or the dress is old or they've gained weight. By the time they have finished running themselves down, the person who uttered the praise regrets having done so.

If you are praised, say "Thank you!" Don't make the other person feel foolish for having complimented you.

Praise: Embarrassing

"Praise in public and criticize in private" has been standard management advice for years and yet it does not work with people who are embarrassed by praise. In addition to the matter of personal preference, some cultures are less comfortable with open praise.

That is why it's important to learn the attitudes and reactions of your employees and co-workers. Tailoring your approach to the individual may seem unduly time-consuming but, when it comes to personal relationships, one size does not fit all.

You should also be wary of over-praising. If everything the employee does is outstanding or great, then nothing is outstanding or great. Too much praise devalues praise. Biographer Joseph E. Persico notes that when Nelson Rockefeller was governor of New York, his habit of inflating praise was so lavish that "You're the greatest" meant you earned a grade of C.

Praise: Irritating

Pretend that you are an administrative assistant. I mention, "Do you know Jack Goodheart? He has to be one of the finest administrative assistants I have ever encountered! He's brilliant!"

You may be thinking, "What am I? Mediocre?"

Praising another can be interpreted as an indirect put-down, much as children may view a parent's praise of the kid down the street as a way of saying, "Why can't you be more like that person?"

There is a Turkish phrase - "May he (or she) be as good as you" - that is used before praising another. It recognizes the very human reaction that may arise when praise is being given to someone else. You don't need to sound so formal, but it is wise to recognize the subtle effects of praising one in front of another.

Praise: Undiluted

If you are going to praise someone, give praise and nothing else. It should not be watered down with qualifying remarks ("For a new employee, Sally did a very good job.") nor should you make your motives suspect by combining it with a request for something. Overstatement is another blunder because it will bring your judgment into question.

Let your praise be direct, credible, and sincere.

A Chief Executive Officer traveled to the outlying locations and spent quite a bit of time in the field. A board member criticized him because of his high travel budget. The response? "You can pretend to care, but you can't pretend to be there."

Sometimes, being there is the most important message. You may not recall what someone said at a family funeral; but you will remember who bothered to show up. When a leader takes the time to get out and talk to people, over 90 percent of the message may be received when the leader appears.

Presumptions: Be Wary of

In working with a very diverse pool of clients and community groups over the years, I've often heard how much people are irritated when others presume that they hold certain opinions or have a particular lifestyle or background. Some examples are when an Asian American, whose family has been here for generations, is presumed to be a recent immigrant; an African American employee is presumed to know other employees of the same race; a Jewish employee is presumed to come from New York; a conservative is presumed to be liberal (or vice-versa); a white employee is presumed to come from a wealthy or a middle-class background; and a young employee is presumed to be a fan of hip hop.

We all make presumptions, but it helps to be wary of them because they can keep us from seeing the beautiful complexity of other people. Pretend that you've just heard about Kathleen, a 33 year old woman who works as a copywriter for an advertising firm in Miami. [Take a moment and think of the flood of presumptions that people might make about her just based on that brief description.]

Now consider the reaction when it is discovered that she is African American, has a house in the suburbs, a golden retriever and a degree in business, loves classical music, hates rap, thinks jazz is okay, is a Cary Grant fan, subscribes to National Review, goes every morning to mass, speaks Spanish, cooks French, has been to Hong Kong twice, volunteers as a docent at a local art museum, re-reads Jane Austen novels, makes a great chocolate mousse, helps out at the food bank, invests in the stock market, cries at the end of Toy Story 3, likes westerns, drives an old Jeep, gets along very well with her parents and her two brothers, and scuba-dives.

And, by the way, she's gay. Is that combination impossible? No. Don't presume too much about the Kathleens of the world.

Profanity, Obscenity, and Other #%*! Things

Sometimes, a bleeping good swear word may exceed the eloquence of more polite phrases but those times are rare. Usually, you diminish your own stature when you resort to such language. Use it frequently and whatever punch it possessed will go down the same drain as your reputation.

One of my favorite examples from history is General Anthony McAuliffe who, when his forces were surrounded by German troops during the Battle of the Bulge, responded to the German surrender demand with the word, "Nuts!" That was much classier than any profanity the General might have uttered.

And how did the great UCLA basketball coach John Wooden swear? "Goodness gracious sake's alive!"

Profanity and obscenity may be as overrated as they are overused.

Religion: Traditional and Otherwise

If you think you know most of the religions out there, think again. Human Resources professionals will quickly tell you of the growing number of new religious denominations that are reflected in requests for reasonable accommodation under the civil rights laws. This increase in religious diversity is illustrated by the fact that, as the Los Angeles Times reported, the United States Air Force Academy has built "an outdoor worship area for pagans and other practitioners of Earth-based religions."

Religious discrimination complaints are also on the rise. American law requires that employers provide reasonable accommodation for religious practices unless doing so would produce undue hardship. It makes sense to tread carefully when the always touchy subject of religion arises and to recognize that snap decisions will not serve you well. The workplace should be a friendly place for believers and non-believers alike.

Results versus Process

Some executives and managers see no problem if the results turned out well. They think Process takes a distant second to Results.

Lawyers and human resources professionals, however, are process-oriented. They can envision a series of disasters if the proper process is not followed. To them, a dedication to process is not inconsistent with a dedication to results because if the process is inappropriate, the desired results are less likely to transpire.

Be alert for these differences when discussing workplace problems. If you emphasize Process to Results people, they may think you're a bureaucrat. If you disregard Process and only emphasize Results to Process people, they may think you're ruthless, unsophisticated or unethical.

Sarcasm: Use of

"You really did a bang-up job on that!"

"Where did you buy your degree?"

Few people can be sarcastic toward others without being destructive.

Your wit may quickly produce a multitude of sarcastic observations, but if you are wise your sense of discretion will stop them before they reach your tongue. As humorous as the remark you're considering is, it may not be worth the collateral damage to feelings and relationships.

Harold's quip that Gretchen's personality couldn't trigger an electric door probably caused a few chuckles but it may haunt Gretchen for years and harm her in ways Harold never intended.

If you are a sarcastic person, I'd love to sit next to you at a dinner party but would prefer that you restrain your wit in the workplace. You may be creating more enemies and victims than you realize.

Sensitive: Being Too

Sensitivity is usually regarded as a virtue, but there are times when it becomes a decided drawback. One of those is when a person reads more into a conversation or remark than was truly intended. For example:

> *"She said she was impressed by Carol's plan. That means she didn't like mine."*
>
> "He said he likes getting out in the field. He must not care for the folks in the head office."
>
> *"She got up to get a cup of coffee during my presentation. She couldn't wait to get out of there."*

The tricky part of sensitivity is that sometimes, it's right! But it can go far astray when the other party is not given to nuance and simply means what was said. There are times when "I don't care for that approach" means just that and nothing more. It doesn't have anything to do with your weight, race, ethnic heritage, personality, parents, children, sex life, neighborhood, pets, or favorite color.

Shots: Cheap

I knew a department director who used to say, "You don't need to be a college graduate to figure that out." He would frequently use that expression in front of a subordinate who hadn't graduated from college. The rest of us suspected the motive behind the remark. Our reaction, however, was probably a little different from the one intended by the department head.

We didn't think he was witty or worldly. We thought he was a jerk.

Cheap shots can be extremely expensive. Without getting into karma, let's just note that people have friends, friends have connections, word gets around, and even bystanders can have long memories. Many a career has been ruined by a cruel joke or a snide remark.

" She complained about my joke? Fine, I just won't talk to her anymore."

That's brilliant. I'm sure that management will be pleased to learn that the original complaint may soon be followed by a retaliation claim.

Grow up and work with the other person, who may or may not be a weasel, in a professional manner. By doing so, you'll gain credibility in the eyes of those who want you to act professionally and you'll frustrate critics who long for you to act irresponsibly so you can confirm their skepticism.

Silence Doesn't Mean Agreement

"We're a pretty rambunctious bunch, but if you ever feel uncomfortable about anything that is said, all you have to do to speak up and we'll back off."

Even if that ground rule is stated with all sincerity, does anyone really believe that people will speak up and reveal their areas of vulnerability? In many cases the person will fear that speaking up will only make matters worse. "I'll be regarded as a prude" or "They'll just say I don't have a sense of humor" are a few of the reasons for remaining silent. Who's to say that those fears are baseless?

It's great if people speak up and give you the chance to correct or prevent offenses, just don't count on it.

To make things even more complicated, some comments, once uttered, can never be taken back. A supervisor who uses a racial slur may find it impossible to regain the trust of the entire team. The only way those disasters can be prevented is by restraint.

Discretion is an underrated virtue. We need more people in the workplace who are willing to embrace the beauty of the unexpressed thought.

Standing Too Close

Cultures vary on how close you should stand when speaking to another person. Some cultures believe you should "bathe in the breath of the other person." Others favor at least an arm's length of distance between the two parties. I suggest an arm's length plus two inches of distance.

Why? Because it is wiser to be more formal than to risk invading another's territory. Unless there is an innocent cultural reason, standing very close is a favorite technique of harassers and intimidators. If you are uncomfortable with a person's distance, it helps to say, "Hold on. I'm one of those people who need some distance. You'll have to back off a bit so I can focus on you."

This can be a great way of determining if the other person does have an ulterior motive. If they continue to stand closer after the warning, you may need to talk to Human Resources about the problem.

Symbols: Don't Mess With

The flag. The cross. The Star of David. The crescent. All carry special meaning and should be handled with special care. And if you think that message is self-evident, look at how often you can turn on the television for a sporting event and catch professional athletes chewing gum and looking bored during the playing of the National Anthem. Worse yet, consider the uproar sparked when professional football players "took a knee" during the National Anthem.

The minute they began explaining that they didn't mean to be disrespectful or unpatriotic, they were playing defense,

A basic rule regarding symbols: Treat them as if they are nitroglycerine. Be very respectful.

Technical Skills Don't Always Count for Much

I don't care if you are a technical wizard, if it takes your supervisor 40 minutes to persuade you to do something when with anyone else it would take two minutes, your attitude is a performance issue. If your team mates work around you, rather than with you, because you are too gruff or rude or arrogant, then your lack of basic courtesy is affecting the entire workplace.

Unless you work where they can isolate you and slip food in under the door, you've got to be able to work with people. Employers will find it easier to train a person who is technically weak but pleasant than to buy a new personality for someone who is technically strong but abrasive.

Television, Radio, and Books

If you could go back to the Fifties, you'd find that although television, radio, and books were censored, there were not many laws prohibiting harassment in the workplace. [It was not unusual to find cartoons showing the boss chasing his secretary around the desk.]

Nowadays, it has flip-flopped. Employees may drive to work after having watched sexually explicit films the night before and while listening to racy talk by early morning radio crews. Once they arrive at the workplace (and even earlier if they came in on a van provided by the employer), they are in a different, more restrictive, legal environment.

Just because you hear something on television and radio or read it in a best-seller does not mean that the material is appropriate for the workplace. The general culture has a different set of rules.

Terminology: Presumptions

We all presume certain things in order to get through life. Grandparents are presumed to be relatively old. First year college students are presumed to be young. Those presumptions are not always accurate and yet they're usually a safe bet.

Presumptions can expose you to criticism when they carry the potential link to a negative assumption. If you say "policemen" instead of "police officers," you should be prepared for critics who will conclude that you don't favor or can't conceive of women in law enforcement. The same problem occurs with terms such as firemen versus firefighters.

Is "police officer" a better term than "policeman?" I believe so, because it is more accurate. Does that mean that we should immediately chastise anyone who uses "policeman?" Not if we have our priorities in order. Criticizing a person who may well otherwise be a supporter of more substantive efforts on behalf of equal opportunity is sacrificing substance for style. Besides, many terms are used out of habit and not with ill will.

Terminology: What's In and What's Out?

Terminology evolves along with sensitivities. "Guy" has become sex-neutral. (It's not unusual to hear a woman ask her female colleagues, "Are you guys going to lunch?" On the other hand, you don't hear men asking male colleagues, "Are you gals going to lunch?") Terms like "Chicano" drift in and out of popularity.

These changes are yet another reason to cut people some slack. You'll always have some folks who haven't gotten the latest signals. Here are, however, some general guidelines:

African American or Black? Both terms are acceptable and are commonly used.

Hispanic or Latino? Both are fine. Hispanic is still the more popular term. Latino (and Latina) are growing in popularity and may soon surpass Hispanic.

American Indian or Native American? At last count most tribal members prefer "American Indian" although "Native American" is close. You'll encounter tribal members who strongly prefer one term over the other. Asking the person's preference or using American Indian/Native American may be the best approach until the matter is clarified. You may find individuals who prefer that their specific tribal membership be used.

Asian American or Oriental? Asian American is the more popular term. Some critics regard "Oriental" as Eurocentric or even colonialist.

White or European American? Most people use "White." "European American" has not caught on outside of university sociology departments.

Anglo? This term for non-Hispanic Whites is commonly used in the Southwest. It may raise objections from some White ethnic group members, such as Irish, Poles, Slavs and Italians, who do not have British ancestry.

Minorities? This term will have accuracy problems in such states as California as the traditional majority becomes the minority. Some people see it as offensive.

People of Color? This has become the "in" replacement term for "minorities" in some quarters but it has yet to achieve wide popularity, possibly because it sounds like a variation of "colored people." [And does anyone other than the NAACP – the National Association for the Advancement of Colored People – still use that term?]

People of Faith? This term, with its echoes of People of Color, is used to describe religious believers. It is another term that has yet to achieve wide usage.

Sexual Orientation or Sexual Preference? This evokes the question of whether people are born with a particular sexual orientation or choose one. Sexual orientation is the more widely-used and favored description.

Handicapped or Disabled? Most advocacy groups prefer "People with disabilities" because it places emphasis on the person and not the disability. "Handicapped" has become an irritant for many, due to a theory that it stems from the term "cap in hand," which supposedly referred to beggars.

(People who play "Gotcha" assume that "handicapped" is meant to be derogatory. That is ridiculous. Most people who use the term never heard of the "cap in hand" story.)

Territory: It is Wise to Get a Visa

People have their turf, such as their desk, computer, filing cabinet, and chair. Unless you know the person very well, ask permission before encroaching on their territory. This is one of those areas in which formality is best.

It is highly unlikely that a sale has been lost or a relationship damaged because a person respected turf. Remember this before you plop your briefcase on someone's desk.

Thanking People

"Thank you" notes, gifts, and remarks should be uncluttered by any other topics or emotions. If you pack in other topics, the expression can be diluted or tainted.

For example, a young manager thanks a senior executive who is about to move on from the company for the mentoring he has provided over the years. The manager adds, "That's a great company that you're going to. I've always wanted to work there." Oops! What was a nice expression of appreciation suddenly sounds like the calculating ploy of a job-seeker. The moment has been ruined.

When you thank others, stay on topic. Keep your message simple and sincere.

Timing Can Be Everything

A company fired a manager on Take Your Child to Work Day. The child had a vivid introduction to corporate life as dear, old Dad packed his desk contents into a cardboard box and was escorted to the front door by a security guard. The story made the pages of a major business publication and, no doubt, became part of that company's lore.

If you are the bearer of bad news, consider the timing as well as the urgency. It can keep a basic termination decision from becoming a colorful illustration of insensitive management.

Topics: Sensitive

You remember the old admonition to avoid discussing religion and politics? Well, I love discussing religion and politics but they usually aren't great topics when your goal is to bring people together and not drive them apart. Would you advise a company representative to be sure to discuss religion and politics with sales prospects? No way. And yet some people raise those topics with co-workers with scarcely a thought as to whether the discussion will harm teamwork.

What are some other topics that can be especially sensitive? Family, sexual orientation, suicide, abortion, AIDS, intimate health issues, and rape are just a few that may cause embarrassment.

There is an adage, "Never speak of rope in the house of a man who has been hanged." Often, you don't know the backgrounds of co-workers who may be carrying memories and burdens that you'll never suspect. Treading gently or not at all with some topics is a wise course unless you know the person extremely well and are able to discuss the subject without causing offense.

Touching

The company vice president was known as a mad hugger. He would see women and rush to hug them. Some of the employees didn't mind, but others dove through doorways whenever they saw him coming. When he was eventually hit with a harassment complaint, there was no evidence of any groping or fondling and yet he'd failed to apply a basic communication tool, the Platinum Rule: Treat others the way they want to be treated.

The women who didn't like his hugs said, "What am I going to say? He's a vice president!" The mad hugger had to stop his touchy-feely routine and act more professionally.

Can a pat on the back or a hug be appropriate? Sure, but it's not wise to make them a daily routine in today's workplace and they should never include any touching that can in the least way be regarded as sexual or erotic.

Trust

When you strip away many employee relations problems, at the core you'll find a lack of trust. If people trust you, they'll be willing to forgive dumb and thoughtless remarks because they know your heart. If they don't trust you, it is easy for them to suspect bad faith or evil motives.

Stay away from any actions, no matter how small, that will detract from your co-workers' ability to trust you. Go out of your way to be courteous and to show respect.

That's worth repeating: *Go out of your way to be courteous and to show respect.*

Zone of Indifference

Not every remark or action deserves a response. Rather than creating or prolonging an unpleasant situation, it can help to move the conduct and opinions of others into a zone of indifference. You're not saying you approve or disapprove. You are simply adopting an attitude of not caring. Do you really care if one of your co-workers believes that Shakespeare is boring or that "Cannonball Run" is one of the greatest movies ever made?

Obviously, this will not apply to moments when you have an ethical or professional duty to speak up, such as in harassment cases. Putting topics and people into the zone, however, can be liberating. You don't need to bother with every subject. Move the unimportant ones into your zone.

Pushing the Hot Buttons of Groups

It is a bold task to attempt to identify the hot buttons of various groups – issues that arouse special sensitivity – if only because the groups and their members are extremely diverse. It is possible, however, to identify three broad categories that contain danger zones that one should be on the watch for with any group: History, Stereotypes, and Current Events.

History. Remarks that are insensitive to the historical suffering of groups can trigger especially stern reactions. African Americans are understandably alert to any comment or behavior that makes light of or diminishes the significance of slavery and segregation. When some college fraternity holds a "slave auction" at a party and then tries to explain that it was referring to Greek slavery, and not anything in the American experience, the fraternity is hard pressed to downplay what references to slavery mean in the United States.

Failure to pay sufficient deference to the pain of a historical wrong, such as slavery, Jim Crow laws, the Holocaust, Wounded Knee, Pearl Harbor, September 11, and other events, is practically asking for controversy. People will not "get over" such events because they logically believe that certain matters should never be forgotten. Such events will always be an open wound.

Stereotypes. Some stereotypes are harmless. The French do like wine. The Germans are efficient. Parties in Greece and Italy will probably be livelier than those in Finland. Other stereotypes, however, can harm. This group or that one is lazy, treacherous, irresponsible, violent, cold, untrustworthy, selfish, corrupt . . . well, the list can go on-and-on. Any remarks that have the slightest connection with a negative stereotype, such as all Italians are connected with the Mafia, the Irish are a bunch of drunks, women are weak, Poles are dumb, Southerners are prejudiced, New Yorkers are rude, and old people are senile, will draw an unpleasant reaction. [Lest you think that harmful stereotypes are a thing of the past, see how often television commercials portray men as sports-addicted, beer-swilling, romantically awkward oafs.]

As mentioned earlier in the book, we have generations of young people – and more than a few older ones – who are not aware of the negative stereotypes that were historically used to oppress and harm various groups. As a result, you may find a young person who does not know that there used to be racist cartoons depicting

Blacks stealing chickens and eating watermelon. It helps if that person learns more about the potential historical sources of offense, but it also makes sense to recognize that many people do not know of those negative stereotypes and therefore intend no offense.

Current Events. List some current events which, in addition to being sensitive, can be of special interest to various groups: Immigration, terrorism, English language requirements, prayer in public schools, Affirmative Action quotas, gay marriage, multiculturalism, AIDS, Israel, gun control, and health care are just a few.

Comments that relate to a matter of public controversy will draw attention because of the obvious: they relate to a matter of public controversy. It is rather sad that we have gotten to the point where people feel compelled to go through a litany of disclaimers to state what they are not saying before getting to the point they wish to make. This is done in part for clarity's sake and because those who are prone to find insult may want to associate the remarks with more extreme or distasteful positions; a form of guilt by ascribed association.

Some Closing Points

Part of the reasoning behind this book is that if you want to be provocative or controversial, you should at least do so knowingly. John Wayne once said that his father taught him never to insult anyone unintentionally. Those who balk at suggestions that remarks should be tempered should at least keep that rule in mind. Why harm those whom you do not wish to harm? Why inadvertently create a communication barrier and damage your reputation?

My final recommendation is the foundation for all that has been mentioned earlier. The key to a successful workplace and a good reputation is the fostering of trust. Remarks that cause others to doubt you, and which consequently erode the ability to trust, can significantly affect the strength of your team. They can weaken your ability to do the job. They can seriously damage your career and standing in your organization and even in the community.

To one extent or another, all of us are diplomats. The extent to which we fulfill that role can determine how far we rise. Don't dismiss the importance of your diplomatic responsibilities. There are some rare exceptions, but most individuals who move up in life have mastered the ability to get along with others and to defuse problems rather than stir up needless controversy. Regardless of your job title, you are an Ambassador of Good Will both within and outside of your organization.

Choose your words accordingly.

About the Author

Michael Wade is a management consultant with Execupundit Consulting, LLC in Phoenix, Arizona. Prior to starting his consulting practice, he served as the EEO Administrator for the City of Phoenix and as the Command Equal Opportunity Officer for the United States Army Criminal Investigation Command in Washington, D.C. He has advised corporate executives, police and fire chiefs, city managers, Army generals, professional athletes, and entry-level employees on sensitive issues. He writes the Execupundit.com blog and is a popular speaker.

The author of several books, he holds degrees in government and law from the University of Arizona. He may be reached at michael@execupunditconsulting.com.

www.execupunditconsulting.com